Adventures With StampyCat: A Fiction Novel

Jacob E. Jones

D1417412

Disclaimer

Legal Disclaimer

Table of Contents

Chapter 1

Stampy slowly looked around from side to side. The same view of the forest began making him sick.

He saw the same view every single day. He wanted to see the whole world, but he was stuck looking at this forest.

His sister warned him the dangers that were lurking completely outside the forest.

Nelly was a cat just like Stampy was. However, her fur was a bright pink color. She was afraid of all the things that Stampy wasn't scared of.

She was afraid of Zombies, Spiders and all types of other things. She jumped whenever she heard the smallest noise in the distance.

Stampy slowly sighed. While Nelly was sleeping, he got some

belongings and set off looking for an adventure. He wanted to find a place where he would belong.

The sun was just rising when Stampy had left. He was nowhere to be seen afterwards. Nelly soon woke up and saw that Stampy had left.

She began struggling in her mind. She paced back and forth trying to think of what to do.

Should she go and find her brother? She didn't have much of a choice.

She could both stay and worry or she could go looking for him.

She grabbed some torches and a sword before heading out to look for Stampy.

Chapter 2

Nelly called out, "Stampy!"

She walked out of the forest towards the clearing. She heard no reply though. The wind wasn't even rustling the trees as she continued to walk.

The sun was now high in the sky and Nelly could not find her brother.

She began crying and a

bird landed next to her. The bird said, "What is wrong?"

Nelly looked at her. She slowly said, "I am looking for my brother."

She replied, "Who? The golden-cat?"

Nelly nodded, "Have you seen him?"

The bird shook her head. She slowly said, "I always see you in the forest. I was wondering when you were going to finally leave."

She laughed and said, "My name is Zoey. How about you?"

She said, "My name is Nelly!"

Zoey said, "If you would like, I can help you find him."

Nelly looked at her and said, "You will help us?"

Zoey said, "Of course!"

Nelly jumped up and hugged her. She said, "Thanks!"

As the sun began setting, they continued walking forward in search of Stampy.

Chapter 3

Stampy continued walking on. He knew Nelly would eventually come looking for him, but he just wished to be free. He finally had the freedom he was looking for.

He had wanted this for a very long time, but he still felt guilty about doing it. Everything was extremely peaceful.

Suddenly, Stampy saw someone dressed in yellow and red with a mustache walking towards him.

Stampy slowly walked away from them. The sun began setting and the moon slowly started rising now. It was a full moon during this night.

The person said, "Don't be scared."

Stampy asked, "Who are you?"

The voice said, "I'm Ty."

Stampy said, "Nice to meet you. My name is Stampy!"

A wolf slowly began walking up towards them. Stampy got a bone and he gave it to the wolf. After a short amount of time, they became friends.

Stampy slowly said, "I will call you Greg!"

Greg jumped around happily and Stampy tied a red scarf around his collar.

Greg loved this idea and he jumped around for a bit. Ty stared at both of them. He got a mob whistling and calling out towards them.

Greg stopped jumping and suddenly began growling viciously at the bushes and trees. Stampy looked around, but he lost Ty.

Skeletons drew back and began shooting arrows towards Greg and Stampy.

Stampy shouted, "Dodge the arrows Greg."

However, it was far too late. An arrow struck Greg and killed him on the spot as he collapsed.

Light came and all the skeletons burned, but Stampy began crying. He

lost a really good friend
of his own.

Chapter 4

Ty came out and said, "Leave them be!"

Stampy asked, "Where did you go? Why didn't you help us?"

Ty said, "I was busy!"

He didn't want the dog to die but rather Stampy.

Stampy stood up and began walking away. Ty then said, "Where are you going?"

Stampy didn't reply, he just ran. He ran so quickly that he didn't notice the large squid right in front of him.

The squid said, "Can you not see where you are going?"

He grabbed his hat and dusted the dirt off of it.

Stampy slowly said, "I'm sorry. My name is Stampy!"

He said, "Mr. Squid."

He stood up and said, "You seem to be in a real hurry to go somewhere." Stampy said, "Oh no. I'm a little bored."

Mr. squid said, "Bored? Come with me then!"

Stampy asked, "Where are we going?"

"You will see!"

They both walked on together.

In the meantime, the night for Zoey and Nelly was horrifying. Spiders, skeletons, creepers, and zombies came at them from everywhere.

They had to run throughout the night to survive until it was morning.

Zoey asked, "Nelly?"

Zoey said, "Are you sure there is any point searching for him?"

"We are family, we have to help one another!"

"Okay, if you say so."

Suddenly, a giggling could be heard in the distance. They walked towards the area where the sound came from.

Nelly said, "Come on Zoey!"

"Fine!"

They both walked towards the girls and they looked up to them. The girls both said, "Who are you?"

"I am Nelly and this is Zoey!"

"My name is Amy and she is Rose."

Rose asked, "Where do you think you're going?"

Nelly said, "We don't know to be honest. We

are trying to find my brother."

Rose said, "Stay here for a bit. You both seem scared."

They agreed and stayed in the area for a bit.

Chapter 5

Mr. Squid and Stampy began walking together. The more that they talked, the more they became friends with one another.

Stampy continued looking around at the strange terrain. Everything was extremely strange.

Stampy felt bad that he left his sister behind. However, he realized he had to do it otherwise he wouldn't be free.

Stampy still wondered whether or not he made the right decision about his sister.

Mr. Squid asked, "Are you ok?"

Stampy nodded and said, "Yeah. I'm just thinking."

Mr. Squid asked, "We are almost here!"

In the meantime, Zoey asked, "Nelly. Are you sure you would like to stay here for a while?"

"Yes. That's fine, but we need the rest."
Nelly began looking around. Amy and Rose were still playing with these flowers and the sun had begun setting.

Nelly felt that someone was watching her. She shook off the thought.

She loved her brother and she couldn't give up.

The moon rose high up in the sky and the sun had now disappeared.

Rose said, "I will patrol."

She grabbed her iron sword and stood by it. Nelly and Zoey felt safe and fell asleep.

Nelly got up and realized that they had both left. She couldn't believe that

Rose and Amy would leave like that.

Nelly said, "Wow. Leaving without telling us a thing!"

"Come on Zoey. No point of staying here, lets go!"

Chapter 6

Stampy continued traveling through the plains biome. They had been walking since yesterday and Stampy didn't know where he was going.

From a tree far away, Ty watched them slowly. He had a pack of wolves together that were full of evil intention.

He ordered the wolves, "Go!"

They sprinted towards Stampy and his new friend. They noticed the wolves coming from all sides.

They pulled out their swords. Mr. Squid said, "Whatever you do, do NOT allow them to bite you."

They took their swords and began stabbing them as quickly as they could. However, the last of the wolves turned towards

Stampy and began attacking him.

Mr. Squid said, "Hurry. We can still help you!"

Mr. Squid carried Stampy and rushed forward hoping to save his life.

Mr. Squid left Stampy hidden in the trees. Rose walked by and asked, "What is wrong with him? Who is he?"

Squid did not answer. He was concerned about Stampy.

"Amy and I passed by a blue bird and pink cat the other day. The names were Netty and Zoey."

Squid didn't take notice to do this. She said, "The cat reminds me a lot of the girl cat I saw yesterday."

After a few minutes, Squid came back and he had a potion in his hand.

Rose said, "What happened?"

"Evil wolves came and attacked us."

Mr. Squid shook his head and he handed him the potion hoping to wake him up.

Stampy finally opened his eyes.

Mr. Squid shouted, "Stampy!"

Stampy asked, "What happened?"

Mr. Squid said, "Do not worry about what happened."

Stampy looked at them and smiled. Rose then said, "I still don't get what happened."

They looked at her. They asked, "What do you have to say?"

"We were playing in the forest when a pink cat and bird appeared."

Stampy was stunned. He sat up quickly. He knew it was his sister when they mentioned the pink cat.

Stampy quickly asked, "Where at?"

"A tiny clearing in the woods, why do you ask?"

Stampy said, "Oh. Just wondering!"

His sister was now getting closer and he knew he had to do something. The pressure was intense since Ty was also watching him and trying to kill him at this time.

Chapter 7

Nelly walked on continuing to look at everything. Zoey however was tired from walking through this.

Zoey said, "Take a rest Nelly!"

Nelly replied, "I know he has been here and I want to find him."

Nelly picked up the leaves, looked at them and began smelling it.

She could tell from each of the leaves that Stampy had been there.

Ty saw her and he knew exactly who it was. He jumped right in front of them and Nelly was terrified.

Ty said, "Don't be scared."

He grabbed the evil wolf by the collar. Nelly picked up a stick and pointed it straight towards them.

Nelly asked, "Who are you, what are you doing here and what do you want?"

He said, "I'm Ty!"

Zoey asked, "Nelly. Can we go?"

Nelly said, "Yes. Please!" Ty walked creepily as they both walked away.

Stampy was now with Rose after she wanted to stay with him. Rose found her chance to finally ask him.

Rose said, "Stampy. Why were you scared when I said I saw a pink cat?"

Stampy asked, "Why do you wish to know?"

"Well she was looking for her brother and I thought you were her brother." Stampy said, "Yes. I am her brother but I refuse to go back to that forest."

"Why don't you tell her that?"

"She is afraid of everything and afraid of being alone."

Rose said, "She can live with you."

Stampy laughed and said, "No!"

Rose didn't understand what was happening. She sighed.

She then said, "Amy and I have some stuff to see. Do you want to come with us?"

"No. I'd rather watch the sun set."

"Suit yourself then. We will be getting the wolves."

Stampy said, "Fine fine. Wait for me. I'll come!"

Rose took Stampy to the crowded places with the

trees. Stampy asked,
"This isn't a forest right?"

Rose shook her head. She
said, "No. It's the
jungle."
Amy stood and admired
all of the trees. Amy then
said, "I was wondering
when you would come.
Rose, it's already
nighttime!"

Rose said, "Sorry Amy!"

They heard a howl and
some rustling noises in
the bushes. Three wolves

walked out and they began walking towards Stampy.

Amy said, "They like you a lot!"

Stampy bent down and gave them some bones. They became friends instantly just like they did with Gregory.
All of a sudden, Ty walked out. Stampy got up and then the wolves began growling towards Ty.

Only one wolf remained with Ty at the moment. Stampy said, "It was you. You are the one who sent those wolves."

He replied and said, "Me. Yup!"

The flowers near the trees began shriveling up. This made Amy extremely angry.

Amy asked, "What do you want?"

He grinned and said, "Oh nothing at all!"

Chapter 8

Ty came out and said, "Leave them be!"

Stampy asked, "Where did you go? Why didn't you help us?"

Stampy began hissing towards him. Amy slowly said, "We need to get out of here!"

However Stampy didn't take notice. He continued glaring at him intensely.

Stampy was getting ready to charge right at him, but Rose held him back.

Rose then said, "Stampy. Come on. Let's get out of here!"

Stampy went forward with them while the wolves followed them.

Nelly said, "Zoey. I know he has been here!"

"How can you be sure? He might not even be close."

Nelly said, "I can just feel it."

Zoey laughed and said, "I can feel the wind!"

Nelly recognized one of the voices in the distance. She knew it was Stampy's voice.

She came and tapped him on the shoulder. Stampy was terrified to see her.

They all turned around. Stampy looked at her

with horror, he really didn't want to go to the forest.

Nelly said, "Stampy. Why did you go?"

Stampy said, "I really didn't want to stay there anymore."

"Why?"

"Because I just didn't."

"But you are here now. That's all that matters now!"

She hugged him tightly.

Ty said, "Oh, how cute. What a nice reunion."

He jumped out of the bushes and grabbed a bow and arrow and pointing it towards Stampy.

Chapter 9

Rose leaned over towards Amy and said, "Get the rest of the group quickly!"

She whispered and Amy jumped into the pool of the water and began swimming away.

Stampy shouted at Ty and said, "What do you want?"

Ty replied, "I want to kill you."

He shot the arrows towards her, but it missed him by an inch.

Rose got out some iron swords and handed it to everyone.

Ty said, "A battle? Bring it on!"

Stampy went straight towards them with the weapons and thought it was time to fight.

They charged him and eventually destroyed him. He dropped all of his items and ran off in the distance.

They knew he would return, but they were safe for now.

17546140R00035

Made in the USA
San Bernardino, CA
13 December 2014